Winter Musings

Edited by
Emily Vanseizenberg

Written by
Poetry City Members

First published by
Poetry City Books, United Kingdom
© Poetry City Books, 2024

The right of all featured poets to be identified as the authors of this work have been asserted by them in accordance with the Copyright, Designs and Patents Act of 1988.

Cover photo © James A. Donovan, 2024.
Book design and layout © Emily Vanseizenberg, 2024.
First published in 2024.

All rights reserved. Except as permitted under current legislation no part of this work may be photocopied, stored in a retrieval system, published, performed in public, adapted, broadcast, transmitted, recorded or reproduced in any form or by any means, without the prior permission of the copyright owners.

ISBN: 9798346155997
Imprint: Independently Published

Contents

Foreword

Let Winter In by Emily Vanseizenberg

Dancing Christmas by Joseph Gallagher

The Devil's Greatest Plan by Jennifer J Wilson

Winter Forms Behind Glass by Jaonii

Soldiers by Tim Queen

Little Solstice by Steve Murray

At Your Feet; The Lamentations! by Chuma Ozemene Ndubachibogu

Solitary Ember by Bob W Christian

Christmas Jigsaw by Emily Vanseizenberg

Beautiful! by Jennifer J Wilson

Away in Storage by Joseph Andrew Miller

Tears Fall on Christmas Day by Jaonii

Homeless by Tim Queen

Oh, My Lonely Soul by Pen Blood

During Christmas, When I Was Young by Chuma Ozemene Ndubachibogu

A Mind of Winter by Joseph Gallagher

My Longing for Freedom by Jaonii

Yule by Bob W Christian

Eternal Bonding by Pen of Universality

So by Tim Queen

Ev'ry Christmas by Jennifer J Wilson

In Awe, The New Year Expectations by Chuma Ozemene Ndubachibogu

Falling Together by Emily Vanseizenberg

Some Holiday Drive on the Outskirts of Adolescence by Joseph Andrew Miller

Index, Acknowledgements and More Information

Foreword

Welcome to the first Poetry City poetry anthology and thank you for purchasing a copy of this book.

Ten members of the Facebook group Poetry City have contributed their original poems to this collection. This book will be listed for minimum listing price on Amazon and no royalties will be earned from the sales of this book – this has purely been published to showcase the talent of our members and for us to have a physical product to look back on.

The poetry in this collection is written in various styles and covers several themes including winter traditions, winter weather, loneliness and other similar topics.

I would personally like to thank everyone who has contributed their poems to this venture and everyone who buys this book – it is all very much appreciated.

I hope that you enjoy reading this collection as much as we have enjoyed creating it.

- *Emily Vanseizenberg, founder of Poetry City*

Let Winter In

Once again, the Winter begins
but I'm reluctant to let her in.

I've missed hot cocoa
and iced mince pies,
but never the dark
and the cold of the nights.

I've missed watching snow fall
from the sky while inside-
but never the walks
or delayed bus rides.

I've missed coming home to
the lit Christmas tree-
but not the stress
decorating gives me.

I've missed Christmas music
but not in November.
Carey and Bublé
belong in December.

But I know that I must let Winter in,
for the festive season is about to begin.

© *Emily Vanseizenberg*

Dancing Christmas

Somewhere between 80 and 90 degrees the trees
Start blooming edible ornaments. Silver figs,
Gold and green apples, alabaster pears,
Cherries, everywhere of red and pink...
The Buddha's favourite colour. Both he and Krishna
Thought it sublime.
Pink was invented by Hieronymus Bosch in 1509.

Until Bosch's " Garden of Earthly Delights",
Pink did not exist in its present form...
Oh, there was Perugino rose,
A Botticelli pale cherry, a Leonardo blush,
But before Bosch's otherworldly carapaces,
Giant birds, cherries, plums, apples, pink
Had never been thought, I think.

Christ himself was robed in blue,
With a gold nimbus and a bunch of depressed
Disciples hanging around, no surprise there,
Betrayal, crucifixion, Golgotha, thorns...
But Bosch's Christ is in pink, his men
And woman embracing giant strawberries
Kissing and consorting with mermaids,
Catching a ride on shiny flying fish.

It's as if Christmas had become a dance
Of whirling dervishes,
My kids and I leaping about like marionettes
With our strings cut, making our tired bones
Loose in their sockets,
We're going to move it; we're going to rock it.

Our feet are religious, our knees like holy water,
Head's crazy with hair, the drumbeat, guitar,

The snare... The Comanche word for themselves
Means Human Beings...
And that's all we are, besotted and beautiful,
Devotees of the Dance.

© *Joseph Gallagher*

The Devil's Greatest Plan

The Devil came up with a grand old plan,
An ingenious way to pit man against man.
He found a way to change man's basic needs
Into nothing more than contempt and greed.

He laughed and laughed 'til his sides were sore,
Why hadn't he thought of this curse before?
There'd be mortals stalking with craze in their eyes,
With nothing in mind but to seize the first prize.

There'd be stomping and tromping, races, disgust,
People feeling malice, no one they could trust.

He kicked back and smiled, "Ah, this is MY day!"
But for those on Earth, I'll call it "Black Friday!"

© *Jennifer J Wilson*

Winter Forms Behind Glass

I admire the winter weather,
I love it when it snows.
I follow each white splinter
As it dances to the ground.
I see myself dancing under streetlamps
along with the little specks of glitter,
The most peaceful dance in the warmest of arms,
Twirling with the direction of the snowfall,
Feeling the gentle grace of each snowflake in my hair -
A moment you'd pay thousands to have bottled in a dome,
An eternity captured in the snow globe on your shelf.

© *Jaonii*

Soldiers

we are
the early stars

of midnight
take my hand and

we can low crawl
 into history

see... breathing
is

an act of courage
it's Rachel's

lost dream
of 'ever after"

listen.

together
we can fight

the little wars
of morning

capture the truth
with the blues

in our pockets, we'll

carve our initials
in the front door

of heaven

every song will
know our name.

© *Tim Queen*

Little Solstice

Full moon waxing a limitless sky
To the inclement season we say goodbye
A solitary witch preserves and takes stock
Our personal fire to our hearts we unlock

With celebration we crest the sky
A shadowy bird clouds that make us cry
Weaving garlands and making prayers
Potent we charge in the fire of many layers

Down river we float uninhibited and free
Circle tradition hen the sun shines so easily
Master and servant my not succeed
Hunters will hunt and keep what they need

© *Steve Murray*

At Your Feet; The Lamentations!

At your feet; the lamentations!
I'm bundled, dropped and dumped
Father! Your eyes, though the eagle's.
Ever living, ever potential ever essential
Watches, while I seem to be washed away
Crying my eyeballs in ever bulging alacrity
My eyebrows soaked in the ever-raining oil.
Tick fluid - creamy chalk liquid
Held to be mere tears
The weight within me, I alone could tell

At your feet; the lamentations!
My entire being by the initial revelation thrown
Landing on your feet I deemed myself fit

The challenges taken
The barton transferred

The mantle accepted
My broad heart opened; my arms spread
Accepting the slot, waking up to the confrontation
The movement;
That clarion call for identity, thus began

At your feet; the lamentations!
The Oba ritual done
That prestigious height attained, for you, a seat secured
You, on that ancestral stool seen sat
And in comfort too
Then the call for a befitting funeral
This, we - the living and the dead - rallied round to achieve
We did, and it was a success
On sands of time, your name written
On marbles of time, your name engraved
The jingles on the streets heard for you

At your feet; the lamentations!
Your lamentations my father I heard
My lamentations to you I'm now handing over
Your place within your ancestors I've restored
My own place in the living, on your feet, my father I seek

Where's your sanity?
Where's your integrity?
Where's your security?
Where's your strength?
Where's your sainthood?

At your feet; the lamentations!
Yes! Question on question
Question upon question
Amidst tears, gnashing of teeth
Mockery, molestation and rejection
Poverty and wretchedness naming
degradation and more
Only the rewards?

Entrapping myself in stagnancy; inactive
and in rottenness
In shut of words, my father
At your feet; my lamentations!

© *Chuma Ozemene Ndubachibogu*

Solitary Ember

In the chill of December, the world is cloaked in twinkling lights,
Streets alive with a warmth I long to touch.
Yet I drift as a lone whisper,
A shadow at the edge of bustling crowds.

The air buzzes with togetherness,
But the echoes of my own silence are deafening.
A stark reminder that solitude is a song
I've learned to sing, though my heart aches to join the harmony.

Families huddle like stars in a constellation,
While I wander alone, an isolated comet,
Seeking a universe to belong to,
Dreaming that one day, my voice will find its place.

Laughter floats in the frosty air,
And I watch, an observer of happiness,
Longing to be part of the joyous chorus,
To bask in the glow of shared moments.

For now, I am a single flame in a window,
Flickering with the hope that someone will notice,
And understand the quiet beauty
Of the glow of my solitude.

© *Bob W Christian*

Christmas Jigsaw

I'll decorate my Christmas tree,
then enjoy a festive shopping spree.
I'll wrap up warm, there might be snow.
I'll paper these presents and tie on a bow.

It's almost time for the big day,
where all the family comes to stay.
It's Christmas now, everyone has arrived,
but tears are forming in my eyes.

Someone is missing, we're not all here.
I am still grieving, and that is clear.
I'm grateful for those who I still have,
but missing the one that's sadly passed.

There's a space where my jigsaw piece should be,
I miss all the complete memories.

© *Emily Vanseizenberg*

Beautiful!

Time erased us,
Like two snowflakes vanishing
When they hit the earth.

We were beautiful,
But the world never knew we existed…
Young, free, falling.

We left not a trace
In time or space,
Just falling … gently falling.

But I remember you,
Holding a moment in time
And you were beautiful, just beautiful!

© *Jennifer J Wilson*

Away In Storage

We sat there in a festive glee
As gifts were passed around
To grasping hands
To gasps of delight and awe
I received my large, unwieldy gift
The corners of my eyes, crinkled as the paper
The corners of my lips, curled as the ribbon
I recited the script of gratitude
But I did not feel it
As I tore off my wrapping of resentment
It didn't matter what it was
What I wanted was to be like everyone else
For my smile to be real
For my heart to be so full of peace
Instead, sat there with my crafted, plastic face
My crumpled self-pity
Kicked under the couch
With the other holiday litter
We said goodbyes and gave our hugs
And I was left to sit back on the floor
Taking off my costume of joy
Not playing with the lowly but thoughtful toy
Even with its sheet of bare instructions

Wondering why there were no instructions
For my straining heart
But I did put the gift in the attic
Where it sat for years
Under a quilt of guilt and dust
Waiting
For the day I will brush it off and try
I will try, I will try, to find true love for it
That I haven't yet learned how to give

© *Joseph Andrew Miller*

Tears Fall on Christmas Day

This Christmas,
We grieve as heavy as a blizzard,
Tears spitting in every direction like a firework to a flame,
We grieve.
Our families finding home in places we cannot see,
Searching for the love we cannot feel,
Vacant spaces at the dining room table,
We certainly grieve.
Stars losing their twinkle,
Corners of the room closing in as we close ourselves off to the idea of healing.

Christmas is not Christmas.
It's just another sad cinematic ending.

© *Jaonii*

Homeless

  we was drankin'
  and sangin'.

wuddint thankin'
about cryin'

or worryin'
 about dyin'.

we was dancin'
'neath the

arms of the trees.
we was sailin'

 a doldrum breeze.
we were the

universe
and

no one
asked any

questions.

© *Tim Queen*

Oh, My Lonely Soul

Oh, my lonely soul
Who can fill your void,
My days on earth are but blank
Empty spaces stare back at me
Some with words I could never read
Some with dreams I could never reach
I'm but a dreamer, a wandering dreamer.

In love I'm but a stranger
In dreams I'm but a mirage,
These words stem from deep within
They seek a soil to take root in
From my birth I sought meaning
A vain thing I kept searching
From these spaces scars appear

Scars mostly self-inflicted
I dream of beauty, I dream of peace
Yet all I see are empty walls
The only thing that's left are shadows
Shadows of what I used to know.

Oh, my lonely soul
When would you find company,
Your spirit longs to be in the light
Where are your smiles
Where are your words
Silver tongues are what you were blessed with
Your words are like music
But your orchestra never played
Your voice was like thunder
But alas it never was heard
From you inspiration flowed
Yet your muse flees
Who can make this emptiness flee
I ask you oh my lonely soul.

© *Pen Blood*

During Christmas, When I Was Young

The journey of that dry cold wind
From the northern hemisphere
On us, huddling, curdling, caressing and kissing
Our eyes deeming, weak and winking
Our skins, drying and shrinking
The air filled with life but dry
Warmth within our bodies asking for more
All around, and surrounding us, the harmattan sings
During Christmas, when I was young

I often hang my ears in the air
Were, throughout the air, on air
The jingles emanate
Fresher and holier, the sweet sonorous festive songs would stand
A harbinger, a messenger, a bringer of those good tidings
Oozing from our radios, televisions and newsprints
Men would begin to, but assimilate and wear good looks
During Christmas, when I was young

The local markets would, but resurrect
Celebrating newest things.
The children's toys, cloths and wares
All, in our markets dancing, flying and landing
Every ware having a mouth to talk, to sing and to walk
Foods, foreign and local would, but have limbs to walk
Walking into the marketplaces
Walking back to new homes
Life rejuvenated, hopes resurrected
During Christmas, when I was young

We would walk, joyfully into the church
Feeling some strange holy glorified hands
Stretching out to touch us
To bless us
And to lead us to the manger
A new home for the boy god
Up, to the front seats for the innocent us
The angels would sing
The church choir would reciprocate
The priests would bless
On seeing the hands of the church god
Our holy hearts would jubilate
The air would remain pure, real, loyal and royal
During Christmas, when I was young.

Back to our homes
Holiness awaiting, joyfulness in the air hovering
The decorating flowers, hanging and waving
Light of rainbow colours, simultaneously shining
Lightening, brightening and deeming
On our tables, to dine and wine

We would behold, sumptuous and heavenly, our meals
Once in one-year special feast
Throughout this period - festive and eventful
Our lives would be glued to the holiness of the period
During Christmas, when I was young.

© *Chuma Ozemene Ndubachibogu*

A Mind of Winter

You must have a mind of Winter
To survive in a world of ice,
Where the trees with shags of snow
Shiver beneath a moon that glitters
Like broken glass, like shards
Of falling glaciers sliding disconnected
Into boiling seas.

The world is weary.
A victim of domestic violence.
The moon is exhausted,
And everything beneath, beyond
And between is frozen and fragile,
Broken and bereft of false hopes.

No one is coming to save us.
No one is riding in on
"A fine Arab charger, coming
To our emotional rescue."
Certainly not the Stones. They're dying
Like flies, like all the old rocker's
Whose cocaine laden hearts are exploding
Like gasoline fuelled Molotov cocktails,
Or cheap Chinese firecrackers
On a side street of Little Saigon.

You must have a heart of summer
To survive in a world where Tsunamis,
Hurricanes, twisters and floods
Are overwhelming the arteries of the Earth's
connective tissue.
A heart of summer to survive
The overarching evils of ungodly greed
Unleashed daily with the deadly sins
Riding apocalyptic horses of death
Into the valley of poverty and darkness.

Even the horse's scream
" How can hunger consume our children
While sodden money rains from the skies
Of millionaires and billionaires."
You need a mind of Winter,
A heart of summer to survive.

© *Joseph Gallagher*

My Longing for Freedom

Freedom isn't blue skies and yellow beams of sunshine.
Freedom when it initially hits is cold and stale, reflecting what only can be described as a steel boulder.
It's painful. It's taunting and like a puppy, initially uncontrollable.
Freedom is the first breathes you take after running for your life.
Fresh air so alien battering your lungs, each breath feeling the moisture get stripped from your throat.
It's scary.
To have all this space, to be lonely for the first time in years and yet still untangling your arms from your legs and your head from your knees.
It's like a baby deer taking its first steps. The first step is agonising, and every sensation overloads your nerves until you stumble.
You take another step, and it doesn't hurt half as bad, but it's painful.
Freedom is bitter. Like a child spitting out medicine, I spit out the taste of freedom.

Freedom is good for me like medicine is for a sick child, but I'm too naive to understand that spitting out the bitterness of freedom entails drinking the chalice of destruction.
I need freedom in my life.
Can I proudly say today that I am aware that I am free?
I can't say such a thing.
Because although I am free, I am still confined to my cage by invisible strings.
One thing I've learnt about freedom is that it's not always possible to free yourself.
You can't cut the strings if your hands are confined and bound by strings, and no one can do it for you if they are convinced the strings aren't there.
So, you're just left hanging, metaphorically speaking.
Let's reimagine freedom.
Freedom is the stitches holding your wounds together.
You won't always need stitches, so long as you don't keep picking at the wound.
Allow the stitches to hold parts of you together as your body connects to itself again.
Your skin will thank you for it.

You reconnect with yourself, your stitches will gradually fade and become one with the dead skin cell matter.
You'll blink and before you know it, you're healed, and your stitches are gone.
If it wasn't for freedom, I wouldn't have ever known how to piece myself back together again.
Can you help me to be free?

© *Jaonii*

Yule

In the heart of winter, when the world wears a cloak of silence,
And the stars hang heavy in the sky,
We gather around the fire, our breath visible like whispered prayers.
Crackling wood and flickering flames illuminating the shadows of our shared stories.
Yule arrives, the longest night of the year,
A sacred pause: a moment to reflect on the darkened paths we've walked,
The burdens we've carried; the dreams buried beneath frost and snow.

We light candles; each flame a defiant spark against the cold.
A promise that light will return; that the sun will rise again,
As we honour the cycle of life,
The ebb and flow of nature's rhythm,
The ancient dance of death and rebirth.

We weave evergreen boughs, symbols of resilience.
Reminders that even in the harshest of winters, life persists.
Clinging to the promise of spring,
While we adorn our altars with tokens of gratitude,
The warmth of cinnamon, the sweetness of honey,
Our laughter shared over spiced cider.
In this sacred space we come together.
Hands clasped, voices raised - invoking the spirits of our ancestors,
The guardians of the earth.
Calling forth the magic that resides in the stillness,
The whispers of the wind; the heartbeat of the earth beneath the snow.

As the night deepens, we embrace the darkness.
Not with fear, but with reverence,
Understanding that within it lies the potential for growth,
The fertile soil of new beginnings.
The quiet promise that we are never alone.
That we are part of something greater -
woven into the very fabric of existence.
And as the wheel turns, we celebrate the return of the light,
The slow awakening of the sun,
Knowing that in this cycle, we find our strength,
Our hope and the magic that binds us all.

© *Bob W Christian*

Eternal Bonding

Their lives were an indelible imprint.
Forever, etched on the canvas of their souls.
Their meeting was destined by fate.
As they stood together,
Hands intertwined,
Their hearts beating in perfect harmony.
Forging an unshakable union, that would endure through eternity.

Their connection was a sacred tapestry,
Woven from thread of trust,
Laughter, and tears, an exquisite masterpiece, that would remain unfrayed throughout the ages.
Comfort they have discovered, in times of hardship.
Solace, they have found in testimony's abode.
For their destiny is guarded by burning lamps.

In each other's eyes, they discovered a mirrored soul.
A reflection of their deepest longings.
Though death crossed path with them,
Yet he failed,

For their destiny, is guaranteed.
Their bond was a symphony of eternal promise.

Together, they form an unbreakable circle.
A sanctuary, of unconditional love.
Where every moment, was a testament of the power of forever.
Their hearts were two halves of a simple whole.
Reunited across the vastness of existence,
Now beating.
Is one in perfect synchrony.

In the garden of their relationship,
Love blossomed as an eternal flower.
Nourished by the warmth of shared laughter.
And the gentle rainfall of forgiveness.

Their love story was an epic poem.
Written across the stars,
Each verse,
A declaration, of the unwavering commitment.
That would forever be their guarding light.

© *Pen of Universality*

So

the winter morning
arrives on silver breath

of children somehow
all is quiet maybe

muffled winter jackets
a crow kept the clock

the church shivered
and sounded the hour

cars hissed the salted street
some kind of fear winter

symbol of death- a lament
for the loss of colour, the

trees shedding their feathers
the fear that winter knows

your name

© *Tim Queen*

Ev'ry Christmas

You said it snowed ev'ry Christmas in your Chicago.
You fell in love in my Kentucky.
We were like children at nineteen,
Thinking we had grown-up hearts.

I think of you ev'ry Christmas
As I shake my snow globe of memories –
Watching them swirl, sink, and settle
As I reach out to touch your world.

But all I can touch are memories
Of a faraway long-ago time
When it snowed ev'ry Christmas in Chicago,
And in Kentucky you were mine.

© *Jennifer J Wilson*

In Awe, The New Year Expectations

In awe
And great anticipation
When we were young
Our hope, enthusiasm and joy
In the air hung
For the great expectations
New year, new resolutions, new life

That bright atmosphere
The Christmas festive feelings
The Christmas trees ornamented in attractive lights
In Manger, that Jesus at the corner welcoming all
The church alters, a heaven drawn to earth and glittering
All hallows in the air hovering
Within and around us would live

It was to
But the Gregorian calendar be honoured
Ushering everyone into a new number count
To the spiritualist, a call for supplications
To the entrepreneurs, crosscheck of the ledgers

To the government, a budget to be made
To us, the children, a time for merriment

The New Year when we were young;
what a reminiscence!

© *Chuma Ozemene Ndubachibogu*

Falling Together

raindrops live short lives.

their skydive lasts
just a few seconds

before they hit the ground,
shards of liquid glass.

at the very least
they fall together,
and don't die alone.

still, I wonder...
does it hurt?

© *Emily Vanseizenberg*

Some Holiday Drive on the Outskirts of Adolescence

a lulling mobile of those sodium-orange lights
on the studded cloth ceiling of a family sedan
returning from somewhere not unimportant
cradled in the sway of switching lanes
bumps on the roadway, a thumping hand
already forgotten, whatever dramas departed
looking at the swinging warm orange glow
and scheming the arrival to home
eyes clamped, feigned sleep
to be carried to bed one last time
they know this con, they don't mind
the weight of change takes this moment
and turns forever those sodium streetlights
into an ache, festive refuse, snow globe flurries

© *Joseph Andrew Miller*

Index, Acknowledgements and More Information

Many thanks to the following poets who contributed to this collection.

Joseph Gallagher

(pages 7-9, pages 27-28)

Jennifer J Wilson

(pages 9-10, page 18, page 37)

Jaonii

(page 10, pages 20-21, pages 29-31)

Tim Queen

(pages 11-12, pages 21-22, page 36)

Steve Murray

(pages 12-13)

Chuma Ozemene Ndubachibogu

(pages 13-14, pages 24-26, pages 38-39)

Bob W Christian

(pages 16-17, pages 31-33)

Joseph Andrew Miller

(pages 19-20, page 40)

Pen Blood

(pages 22-23)

Pen Of Universality

(pages 34-35)

If you enjoyed the work of the above authors and would like to see more, you can find us on Facebook in the group Poetry City.

Poetry City was established in August of 2021. At the time of writing, our group is home to almost 400 members from over 40 countries around the world. This is something we are all very proud of.

We are a warm and friendly community who all share a passion for reading poetry, writing poetry or both. The poetry written and shared by our members covers a wide range of topics and styles, so there is guaranteed to be something for everyone.

Our group also has a weekly newsletter that is shared every Monday. It is used to celebrate the members who have shared their poetry in the last week and to update members on the latest community events.

In the past, we have also offered members several writing prompts and hosted various group challenges which are usually a popular discussion point.

Overall, we are proud to be a friendly and inviting group of poets who regularly share our original poetry, relevant healthy debates and writing prompts.

We hope to create more anthologies like this in the future and to keep sharing our words with the world, as poetry is the one thing that we all share a passion for.

If you would like to join our community, whether it is to read or write with us, just find us on Facebook at the group Poetry City.

To everyone that has contributed to this anthology, that has bought it, shared it, been a part of it. To all Poetry City Members, and to anyone who finds this anthology in their hands. Thank you. Thank you all.

Printed in Dunstable, United Kingdom